the sixties

First published 1985 © International Music Publications
Exclusive Distributors: International Music Publications, Southend Road, Woodford Green, Essex IG8 8HN, England
215-2-274, Order ref: 9910, ISBN 0.86359.267.8
Cover design by Howard Brown/Peter Wood. Photography by Peter Wood

2

ALL I HAVE TO DO IS DREAM

Words and Music
by BOUDLEAUX BRYANT

© 1958 Acuff-Rose Publications, USA
Acuff-Rose Music Ltd, London W1Y 3FA

BORN FREE

Words by DON BLACK
Music by JOHN BARRY

CONGRATULATIONS

Words and Music by
BILL MARTIN AND PHIL COULTER

1. Who would be - lieve that I could be hap - py and con - tent - ed   I used to
2. I was a - fraid that may - be you thought you were a - bove me   That I was

D7   G

think that hap - pi - ness had - n't been in - vent - ed   But that was in the bad old
on - ly fool - ing my - self to think you'd love me   But then to - night you said you

D7   G   E7

days be - fore I met you____   When I let you____ walk in - to my
could - n't live with - out me____ That round a - bout me____ you want - ed to

Am   A7

1   2

heart. _____   2. Con-grat - u -
stay. _____   Con-grat - u -

D7   D.S. al ⊕ Coda

⊕ CODA   Slower   *accelerando poco a poco*

Con-grat-u - la - tions   And cel- e - bra - tions   When I tell ev-'ry-one that

Eb7   Ab   Bb   Bb7   Eb7

Tempo I

you're in love with me ——— Con-grat-u - la - tions   And ju-bi - la - tions

Ab   Bb

I want the world to know I'm hap-py as can be, ——— I want the world to know ——

Bb7   Eb7   Ab   Bb7

— I'm hap-py as can be. ———

Eb7(sus 4)   Ab   G Ab

ALFIE

Words by HAL DAVID
Music by BURT BACHARACH

10

THE CARNIVAL IS OVER

Words and Music
by TOM SPRINGFIELD

DELILAH

Words and Music by
LES REED and BARRY MASON

1. I saw the light on the night that I passed by her win - dow
2. At break of day when that man drove a - way I was wait - ing

I saw the flick - er - ing sha - dows of love on her blind
I crossed the street to her house and she op - ened the door

She was my wo - man
She stood there laugh - ing

FINGS AIN'T WOT THEY USED T'BE

Words and Music
by LIONEL BART

They've changed our lo - cal pal - ais in - to a bowl-ing al - ley, and
mon - keys fly - ing round the moon, we'll be up there wiv 'em soon,

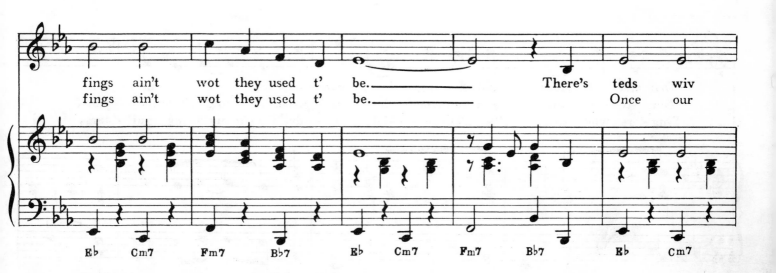

fings ain't wot they used t' be._____ There's teds wiv
fings ain't wot they used t' be._____ Once our

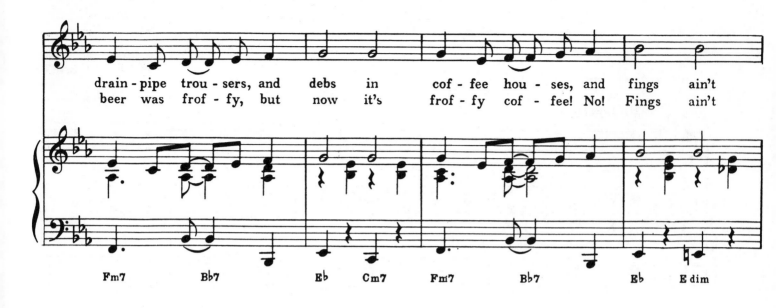

drain - pipe trou - sers, and debs in cof - fee hou - ses, and fings ain't
beer was frof - fy, but now it's frof - fy cof - fee! No! Fings ain't

Fm7   Bb7   Eb   Cm7   Fm7   Bb7   Eb   E dim

wot they used t' be.————— It used t' be fun,
wot they used t' be.————— There used t' be trams,
                          We used to have stars,

Fm7   Bb7   Bbm7   Eb7   Ab

Dad and old Mum pad - dl - ing down South - end, But now it ain't done,
Not ve - ry quick got you from place to place, But now there's just jams,
Sing - ers who sung "A Dix - ie Mel - o - dy," They're buy - ing gui - tars,

Abm

GENTLE ON MY MIND

Words and Music
by JOHN HARTFORD

stashed be-hind your couch.

G7 Dm7 G7 C

— And it's know-ing I'm not shack-led by for-

Cmaj7

-got-ten words and bonds, And the ink stains that have

C6 Cmaj7 C

dried up-on some line,

G9

That keeps you in the back-roads by the riv-ers of my

Dm   Dm(maj7)   Dm7

mem-'ry, That keeps you ev-er gen-tle on my

Dm6   Dm   Dm7   G7 Dm7

1 2 3

mind. ——— 2. It's not

C

4

mind. ———

C

VERSE 2

It's not clinging to the rocks and ivy planted on their columns now that binds me
Or something that somebody said because they thought we fit together walkin'
It's just knowing that the world will not be cursing or forgiving
When I walk along some rail-road track and find
That you're moving on the back-roads by the rivers of my mem'ry
And for hours you're just gentle on my mind.

VERSE 3

Though the wheat-fields and the clothes lines and the junk-yards and the highways come between us
And some other woman crying to her mother 'cause she turned and I was gone
I still might run in silence, tears of joy might stain my face
And a summer sun might burn me 'til I'm blind
But not to where I cannot see you walkin' on the back-roads
By the rivers flowing gentle on my mind.

VERSE 4

I dip my cup of soup back from the gurglin' cracklin' cauldron in some train yard
My beard a roughning coal pile and a dirty hat pulled low across my face
Through cupped hands 'round a tin can I pretend
I hold you to my breast and find
That you're waving from the back-roads by the rivers of my mem'ry
Ever smilin', ever gentle on my mind.

GEORGY GIRL

Words by JIM DALE
Music by TOM SPRINGFIELD

1. Why do all the boys just pass you by? Could it be you just don't
2. Dream-ing of the some-one you could be. Life is a re-al-i-

try, or is it the clothes you wear? You're al-ways
-ty, you can't al-ways run a-way. Don't be so

Eb   Gm   Ab   Bb   Eb   Gm

Ab   Db   Bb7(sus Eb)   Bb7   Bb9   Bb7   Cm

win-dow shop-ping but nev-er stop-ping to buy.
scared of chang-ing and re-ar-rang-ing your-self.

Gm   Ab   Eb

So shed those dow-dy feathers and fly
It's time for jump-ing down from the shelf   a lit-tle bit.

G   C   F   Bb   Bb7

THE GOOD LIFE

Words by JACK REARDON
Music by SACHA DISTEL

love_____ for you can't take the chance,_____ So be

Gb7   Abmaj7   Bbm7 Eb7   Cm7 Ab   C7
                              Gm7

ho - nest_____ with your - self, don't try to fake ro - mance.

Fm   C+   Fm7   Bb7   Bbm7

It's the Good Life_____ to be free___ and ex - plore___ the un-

Eb7   Ab

-known,   Like the heart - aches_____ when you

Gm7   C7   Gm7   C7b9   Fm

GREEN GREEN GRASS OF HOME

Words and Music
by CURLY PUTMAN

green, green grass of home. (2) The

F7   Cm7   F7   B♭   F7

shade   of that old oak tree as they lay me 'neath the

E♭   Dm7 Cm7   B♭

ten.

green, green grass of home.

ten.

rall.

F7   Cm7   F7   E♭   Dm7 Cm7   B♭

VERSE 3. (spoken) Then I awake and look around me
at four grey walls that surround me,
And I realize that I was only dreaming,
For there's a guard and there's a sad old padre
-arm in arm we'll walk at daybreak
Again I'll touch the green, green grass of home.

HELLO DOLLY!

Words and Music
by JERRY HERMAN

I went a-way from the lights of Four-teenth Street And

in-to my per-son-al haze; _____ But

now that I'm back in the lights of Four-teenth Street, To-

mor - row will be bright - er than the good old days!

rit.

Refrain- Medium Strut tempo

HEL - LO, DOL - LY, well, HEL - LO, DOL-LY, It's so nice to have you

a tempo   *mp - mf*

back where you be-long. You're look-ing swell, Dol-ly, we can tell,

Dol-ly, You're still glow-in', you're still crow-in', you're still go - in' strong. We feel the room

35

HAPPY HEART

Words by JACKIE RAE
Music by JAMES LAST

Lyrics:

There's a cer-tain sound___ al - ways fol - lows me a - round,___
Feel - ing more and more___ like I've nev - er felt be - fore,___

when you're close to me___ you will hear it.___
you have changed my life___ so com - plete - ly.___

It's the sound that lov - ers fi - n'lly will dis - cov - er
Mu - sic fills my soul___ now, I've lost all con - trol___ now,

HONEY

Words and Music
by BOBBY RUSSELL

Lyrics:

See the tree, how big it's grown, But
Then the first snow came and she ran

friend it has-n't been too long, it was-n't big
out to brush the snow a-way so it would-n't die

I Came

laughed at her and she got mad, the first day that she plant-ed it was just a twig
run-'nin in all ex-cit-ed slipped and al-most hurt her-self and I laughed 'til I cried

She was al-ways young at heart, Kind-a dumb and kind-a smart and I
Wrecked the car and she was sad and so a-fraid that I'd be mad but

I CAN'T STOP LOVING YOU

Words and Music
by DON GIBSON

Slowly with expression

Those hap-py hours _____ That we_ once knew, _____ Tho' long a-

-go, _____ Still make me blue. _____ They say that time _____ Heals a brok-en

heart, _____ But time stood still _____ Since we've been a - part. _____

IF EVER I WOULD LEAVE YOU

Words by ALAN JAY LERNER
Music by FREDERICK LOEWE

IF I RULED THE WORLD

Words by LESLIE BRICUSSE
Music by CYRIL ORNADEL

IF I WERE A CARPENTER

Words and Music
by TIM HARDIN

find me _____ car-ry-ing the pots I made _____ fol-low-ing be-

-hind me

Save my love through lone-li-ness _____ save my love for sor-row

I've giv-en you my on-li-ness _____ come and give me your to-mor — row _____

If I worked my hands in wood _____
If I were a mil-ler _____

53

I'M A BELIEVER

Words and Music
by NEIL DIAMOND

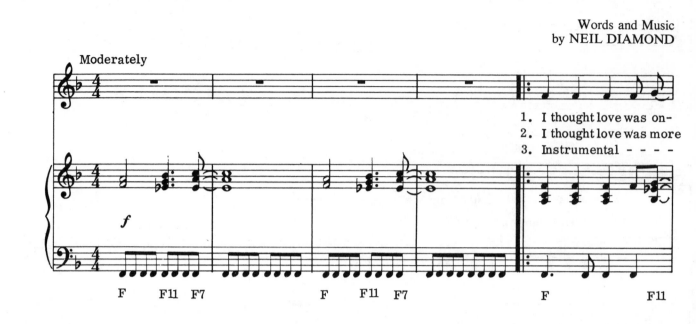

I ONLY WANT TO BE WITH YOU

Words and Music by
MIKE HAWKER and **IVOR RAYMONDE**

58

I on-ly want to be with you. It
I on-ly want to be with you.

You stopped and smiled at me,— Asked if I'd care to dance.—

I fell in-to your op-en arms and I did-n't stand a chance.

Now listen honey, I just wanna be beside you ev-ry-where. As long as we're to-gether honey

I'M COMING HOME

Words and Music by
LES REED and BARRY MASON

THE IMPOSSIBLE DREAM

Words by JOE DARION
Music by MITCH LEIGH

1. To dream the im-pos-si-ble dream, to
(2. To) right the un-right-a-ble wrong, to

fight the un-beat-a-ble foe, To
love pure and chaste from a-far, To

bear with un-bear-a-ble sor-row, to
try when your arms are too wea-ry, to

IT MIGHT AS WELL RAIN UNTIL SEPTEMBER

Words and Music by
GERRY GOFFIN and CAROLE KING

THE LAST WALTZ

Words and Music by
LES REED and BARRY MASON

LITTLE GREEN APPLES

Words and Music
by BOBBY RUSSELL

Sub-published by Peter Maurice Music Co Ltd, London WC2H 0LD

MASSACHUSETTS

Words and Music by
BARRY, ROBIN and MAURICE GIBB

Feel I'm go - ing back _____ to Mas - sa - chu - setts;
Tried to hitch a ride _____ to San Fran - cis - co;
Talk a - bout the life _____ in Mas - sa - chu - setts;

some - thing's tell - ing me _____ I must go
got - ta do the things _____ I wan - na
speak a - bout the peo - ple I have

MAY EACH DAY

Words by MORT GREEN
Music by GEORGE WYLE

Waltz Tempo

MAY EACH DAY in the week be a good day. _____ May the Lord al-ways watch o - ver you _____ And may all of your hopes turn to wish-es_____ _____ And may all of your wish-es come true. _____ MAY EACH DAY in the month be a good day. _____ May you make friends with each one you meet. _____

MY WAY

French Words by GILLES THIBAUT
English Lyrics by PAUL ANKA
Music by CLAUDE FRANCOIS and JACQUES REVAUX

MOON RIVER

Words by JOHNNY MERCER
Music by HENRY MANCINI

ON A CLEAR DAY (You Can See Forever)

Words by ALAN JAY LERNER
Music by BURTON LANE

PUPPET ON A STRING

Words by PHIL COULTER
Music by BILL MARTIN

VERSE

Love is just like a mer-ry-go-round With all the fun of the fair
I may win on the round-a-bout, Then I lose on the swings

One day I'm feel-ing down on the ground
In or out, there is nev-er a doubt

Then I'm up in the air___ Are you lead-ing me on?___ To-
Just who's pull-ing the strings I'm all tied up in you!___ But

-mor-row will you be gone?___
where's it lead-ing me to?___

D.S. al ⊕ Coda

CODA

STRANGER ON THE SHORE

Words by ROBERT MELLIN
Music by ACKER BILK

Moderato (with feeling)

Here I stand watch-ing the tide go out. So all a-lone and blue, just dream-ing dreams of you. I watched your ship as it sailed out to sea, tak-ing all my dreams and

91

TAKE THESE CHAINS FROM MY HEART

Words and Music by
FRED ROSE and HY HEATH

1. TAKE THESE CHAINS FROM MY HEART and set me free ___ You've grown
2. (Give my) heart just a word of sym-pa-thy ___ Be as

cold and no long-er care for me ___ All my faith in you is
fair to my heart as you can be ___ Then if you no long-er

gone but the heart-aches ling-er on TAKE THESE CHAINS FROM MY HEART and set me
care for the love that's beat-ing there TAKE THESE CHAINS FROM MY HEART and set me

93

THERE GOES MY EVERYTHING

Words and Music
by DALLAS FRAZIER

Verse

1. I hear foot-steps slow—ly walk-ing, As they gent—ly walk a-
2. (As my) mem—'ry turns back the pag—es, I can see the hap-py

cross— a lone-ly floor._____ And a voice___ is soft — ly
years__ we had be - fore._____ Now the love___ that kept this old heart

say - ing:___ "Dar-ling, this will be good-bye__ for-ev-er-more."_____
beat - ing_____ Has been shat-tered by the clos-ing of the door.____

REFRAIN

There goes my rea - son for liv - ing,

There goes the one of my dreams, _____ There goes my

on - ly pos - ses - sion, There Goes My Ev - 'ry-

1. thing.
2. As my thing. _____

THERE'S A KIND OF HUSH

Words and Music by
LES REED and GEOFF STEPHENS

TRY TO REMEMBER

Words by TOM JONES
Music by HARVEY SCHMIDT

Moderato

(Slowly, with tenderness)

1. Try to re-mem-ber the kind of Sep-tem-ber when
2. Try to re-mem-ber when life was so ten-der that
3. Deep in De-cem-ber it's nice to re-mem-ber al-

life was slow and oh, so mel-low.___
no one wept ex-cept the wil-low.___
tho' you know the snow will fol-low.___

THE WEDDING

English Lyrics by FRED JAY
Original Words and Music by JOAQUIN PRIETO

Slow Rock

You__ by my side, that's how I see us, I__ close my eyes, and I can see us,

We're__ on our way to say "I do - oo" My__ se-cret dreams have all come

true - oo. I__ see the church, I see the peo - ple, Your__ folks and mine happy and

WORDS

Words and Music by
BARRY, ROBIN and MAURICE GIBB

Smile an ev-er-last-ing smile a smile could bring you near to me ———— Don't
ev-er let me find you gone 'cause that would bring a tear to me ———— This
world has lost it's glor-y let's start a brand new stor-y now my love ———— right

YOU DON'T HAVE TO SAY YOU LOVE ME

Original Italian Words by V PALLAVICINI
English Lyrics by VICKI WICKHAM and SIMON NAPIER-BELL
Music by P DONAGGIO

A WORLD OF OUR OWN

Words and Music
by TOM SPRINGFIELD

Close the door, Light the light, We're stay-ing home to-night. Far a-
love, Oh, my love I cried for you so much. Lone-ly

way from the bustle And the bright ci-ty lights.___ Let them
nights with-out sleeping While I longed for your touch.___ Now your

all fade a-way, Just leave us a-lone___ And we'll
lips can e-rase, The heart-ache I've known___ Come with